DEBORAH UPTON

I0436855

Healing
the Inner Child

Outskirts Press, Inc.
Denver, Colorado

Outskirts Press
http://www.outskirtspress.com

ISBN-13: 978-1-4327-0808-5

Outskirts Press and the "OP" logo are trademarks belonging to Outskirts Press, Inc.

Printed in the United States of America

This book is dedicated to those in my life who have pushed me beyond what I thought I could bear. Because of all the trials and tribulations I have endured, I have found myself in a place of thankfulness. I found myself removed from my comfort zone into a world of confusion and turmoil, which helped me to grow in faith, strength, and my commitment to God. During these trials, I discovered a deeper meaning for my existence, and I discovered my desire to live and make a difference.

Special thanks go out to a very special little boy. You were not on this earth but for a few short months. You never spoke, and never laughed or played; you did not perform any great tasks while you were here, but you, my angel, made a world of difference. Because of your life, and the sequence that followed your death, I was able to find your father. Your dad is a good man who loved you more than life itself. Had it not been for you changing the course of his life we would not be working together for the Lord today.

To my husband, thank you for choosing me. Thank you for loving me when I know it was hard. You believed in me when I did not believe in myself. However, most of all, thank you for hearing God's voice which led you to me. Our ministry will go far if we just remember to keep God first and let Him lead our path.

To my children, thank you for allowing me to love you, and to find joy and love in you. You are the most precious parts of whom I am. God has blessed you both, even before you were born, to do great things. Listen to His voice and let It lead you.

To my precious granddaughter, you are a grandmother's greatest treasure. My heart overflows with love for you, my baby girl, and you make me feel complete and full. I see in you many blessings. You came along during those years when life was throwing me fiery darts and there was no escape. You reminded me how to love, how to dream, and how to want more from this life. Because of you, I have a purpose and a desire to live my life to make a difference in those around me.

To my mother, I think the attached letter, which I wrote to you says it all.

To My Mother:

We often get so tangled up with life that we leave things unsaid which should have been said. I do not want that to be the case with us. We never know what the day may bring or what will happen tomorrow, so we will live each day as though it may be our last.

As a child, I never understood why you chose to remain in the abusive situation we lived in. In addition, I never understood why it seemed that you did not want better for yourself. As an adult, I now do understand those whys. For generations now the women in this family have lived under that curse and never seemed to understand they deserved better. You did not have a very nurturing childhood and I know that had to leave you feeling alone and defeated. You spent a lifetime looking for someone to love you just for you.

Through all your years of struggle, you have managed to raise five "somewhat" wonderful children (especially me). As mothers, we do not always hear much appreciation from our children, nor do we allow much time for our needs and ourselves. I cannot speak for the rest of my siblings only for myself.

I want you to know that I appreciate everything you have sacrificed for us. Because of your choices, I am stronger and able to survive life's battles. Your selfless acts have taught each of us to be more compassionate to those around us. The gift of your heart will be forever treasured, and your love will be passed down to future generations.

We did not always get along, nor were we ever very close, so I am grateful for these past few years of hell. In the ashes of hell's fury, I found the beauty of my mother; a woman I have come to admire and value more than anything else in my life. You have not only become my mother, but you have become my best friend. I truly enjoy being with you and spending time together. Grandma used to call me and get on to me about being so distant, I guess she is happy now. Even in her death, she still has a hand in what happens here.

Always remember that I respect and appreciate you, and that I love you very much. It always amazes me that one single life can change so many others. You, my mother, have allowed your life to change the lives of even those you do not know. I am proud to call you "my mother."

Love always,

Debbie

All names and places referenced in this book have been changed.

INTRODUCTION

This book is a testimonial to those things in my life, which God deemed necessary for my growth. We do not always understand why He trusts us past what we can or will trust ourselves to be able to withstand. As you read these testimonials, God, in all His wonder, never left me even when I did not see Him, and continued to keep His Hand on my life regardless of my decisions or trials. You will finally know and understand that He truly does call us out "even before we were formed in our mother's womb".

My prayer is that if you are reading this you are obviously searching for a sliver of hope in a hopeless situation. You feel that tugging from deep within you that says you know you were called to do more, to be more, and yet you do not understand. You may even feel that no one hears you when you cry silently in the dark. You feel alone trapped in a world, which does not understand you. You may even feel as I did, that you are an alien lost in a world that you do not feel you belong in; a world of strangers and you do not understand why you are here or where your place is.

Let my testimonies remind you of God's love and mercy to see you through what may seem like an impossible situation. If this book were to only touch and change the life of one soul, then all my trials and tribulations made a difference. I am not a martyr and do not seek martyrdom in this. I only seek to allow God to use me to change the heart and direction of one life. Are you that life?

CHAPTER 1
BEGINNINGS

As with any life there must be a beginning. I was born to a woman who had many knocks in life. Her parents divorced when she was young. She did the best she knew how at such a young age to balance between her mommy and daddy as they went about their separate, new lives. As with most young children of divorce she chose paths which were not good for her, and eventually married at an early age. Due to various emotional issues, age and other factors, they soon divorced. They loved each other but did not have the maturity to survive together.

Eventually my mother married again and gave birth to a baby boy two years later. Much to her surprise the man of her dreams, or what she thought was her redeemer, was called to active duty and sent off to war overseas. Now living with her mother, my grandmother, she worked at any job she could find while she waited for her husband to return. I can only imagine how hard this must have been for these two women to live in the late 50's. Working at every menial job they could find to raise this baby alone. My grandmother soon married her knight in shining armor but to her dismay, her husband died of a heart attack within weeks of their marriage.

After a couple of years, the man I was told was my father returned home for a visit and to celebrate my brothers second birthday. But this visit would not be without heartache. During this time he announced to my mother that he had found someone overseas and wanted a divorce. Completely devastated my mother decided not to fight him and honored his request. A divorce was begun. As my mother's life would have it, after the divorce had begun, she discovered that she was pregnant. When my mother was three months pregnant, my dads divorce was granted and he left the state.

Life for my mother and grandmother, now with a two-year-old boy, was hard but they made do. My grandmother was dating a man who was good to them, and life continued. October 1st, 1960 was a day that will never be forgotten in my family. My mother went into labor. My grandmother's boyfriend had stopped by their house to show off his brand new "pink" 1960 Cadillac which he had just bought. He was the only ride to the hospital. He frantically ran around trying to find another way to transport my mother, as he did not want this baby born in his new car. With no other alternative, he reluctantly placed my mother in his back seat, swearing her to promise not to mess his back seat up, and drove as fast as he could towards the nearest hospital.

Arriving at the hospital, while my grandmother ran in for help, he proceeded to fling open the back door of his car, grabbed my mother by her ankles, and started dragging her out of his car screaming "not in my car". You see, she had progressed in her labor very quickly and was yelling, "the baby is coming"! Safely in the hospital, a baby girl was delivered. Feeling alone, unwanted, and without a husband or caretaker, other than my grandmother, with yet another mouth to feed, my mother had not chosen a name for her new bundle of joy, which at that time was not a bundle of joy at all. It was more shame to her because she was an unmarried woman, now with two children to rear alone. At that time, women in her situation were not seen favorably. Hearing that baby cry, in that delivery room, meant even more stress for her. Where would she find food, clothing, and shelter? How would she do this with minimal job skills and resources? What man in his right mind would ever want a woman with two small children? Like most women in her situation, she was scared and felt more defeated and alone than she could bear.

This was not the time to be asking about baby names. However, that is exactly what the hospital staff did. She had not had the time or the convenience of thinking about names during her pregnancy. She had spent her pregnancy in fear, depression, and defeat. At the same moment, a woman in an adjacent room had just given birth to her bundle of joy, which was also a girl. As my mother lay there, tired and terrified, she overheard this woman call her daughter Debora. She looked at the staff and said, "that sounds good to me, call her Deborah". So began my humbled beginnings.

For the first year, I slept in the bed with my grandmother. During that year, my mother reunited with a friend of hers, from her past, and within days of my first birthday married him. My grandmother married a man she had met by the time I reached the age of two, and that is when life as I knew it began and God began His work in seasoning me.

CHAPTER 2
SECRETS NEVER TOLD

My mother and grandmother are two of the strongest women I have ever known. They survived their struggles and now, as life would have it, both had men who were there to save the day. These men would ease some of the burden from them. Much to their surprise, these men would begin even more struggles for these two women, and their children. What lay in wait for them, at the hands of these two men would later be discovered.

My new grandfather was a man of honor in the community. He was a strong family man who devoted his life to helping with his new grandchildren and showing great love to my mother and grandmother. To look at him you would think how blessed my grandmother was for having such love in her life. He loved her, he loved her children, and he especially loved her grandchildren. Grandpa looked for ways to help. On many occasions, he would baby-sit my brother and I to give my mother a break.

I remember the stories of when I was two, my grandfather would baby-sit, and he would boast about all the ways his "little Debbie Do" would make him laugh. On one occasion he was getting me dressed in this little red dress with tiny buttons all the way down the front. I let him button this dress all the way down, placed my hands on my hips, looked at him so innocently, and said, "Grandpa, you put it on backwards with the buttons in the back." The buttons were supposed to be in the front and I had let him put this dress on backwards. He had stood there and buttoned every last one of these tiny little buttons, which was a tremendous feat for him as he was a large man with large hands, 6'1 and 300 pounds.

There were all the cute stories that he told of his little "Debbie Do," but no one knew of the secrets that were held so tight and so deep by this little girl. During the time with the cute little dress with all the tiny little buttons, the desire to explore those forbidden places became so great for this man of honor that he could not resist. Alone with this little girl, looking so pretty in her bare nakedness, he found his hands in places they should not have been. After a while, knowing he was alone in the house with her, he proceeded to climb on top of her. At the age of two, and at the mercy of the man she trusted and loved, childhood as she knew it shattered. Because of his size, and how tiny I was, he was not able to penetrate without causing me extreme pain; after several attempts, he climbed off. Such was the beginning of years of molestation and attempted rapes by this man she loved.

By the age of five, I had discovered a need to protect the rest of my brothers, sister, and cousins from him. I did not understand what was happening but I did know that I did not like it and I did not want it to happen to anyone else. What he was doing to me was making me feel uncomfortable and ugly. I had figured out that if I were there my grandfather would leave them alone and pick me. After all, I did not care anymore and I just figured that it was up to me to save the rest of my family. He continued molesting me until his death when I was sixteen years old. I never told anyone because he would tell me that my grandmother would not love me anymore if I told her. That all I would do is hurt her. My grandmother, bless her heart, went to her grave never knowing because I had vowed never to say anything about what grandpa had done as long as she lived.

I remember his funeral as if it were yesterday. I had dreamed of the day when I was old enough to confront him. I wanted him to tell me why he chose me, and why he would violate my trust. I loved my grandfather because that was what I was taught I should do, but did not understand how he could do those things to me. I did not want to attend his funeral but my step-father decided I had to. He could make me go but not make me go up to his casket, or so I thought. When I refused to go to the casket, he grabbed my ponytail, dragging me up the isle to the casket, shoved my face down on top of my grandfathers chest. I broke free and ran as fast as I could out of the room, crying so hard I could hardly see. I was angry at my step dad for being so cruel. How could he make me touch that man who had hurt me for so many years?

I was very angry with grandpa for dying before I could get my answers. Who in the hell did he think he was? How sick did a person have to be to steal the innocence from such a trusting soul? Did he not realize that that little girl's trust was broken forever, not just with him, but with everyone in her present and future life. Answers I would never have now that he was dead, and yet, relieved that he was dead because his hands would never touch me again and I no longer had to worry about the other children in our family.

CHAPTER 3
DESTINED FOR MENS PLEASURE

My life of sexual abuse did not end with my grandfather's death. I soon discovered that it was the beginning of what was to come for me. Without my realizing it, he had been grooming me for the life I would live. From the age of two, I became every boy and man's playmate. I do not know if it was because I was the oldest girl, or if it was a matter of convenience that I seemed to be the one who was chosen to be molested and abused. Even when my parents moved us to a different state, the abuse continued. From cousins to friends of the family, they all seemed to draw to me for their sexual pleasures. I learned from early in life that it must be normal for girls to go through this, and I must ignore the pain and humiliation I felt. I can remember asking myself if all little girls went through this. Was this how people showed you that they loved you?

Throughout my childhood, I would spend the night with my girlfriends and their brothers would come in to their rooms after the parents were asleep. They would climb into the bed and molest or rape their sister. I remember many times pretending to be asleep hoping they would leave me alone. How could this be wrong if everybody was doing it? Of all the events throughout my childhood, one sticks out in my heart and mind, which was the most devastating to me. It was late fall and my mother was very ill. She had been hospitalized for major surgery and I was left to help take care of my brothers, ages 14 and 10, and sister age 8, help to prepare the meals, and take care of things, after all, I was the prime age of 11 and I thought I was old enough that we did not need help. We went to school by day, road the bus home, and would stay by ourselves until my step dad got in from work.

My stepfather had been raised by violent alcoholics, which predestined him for becoming a violent alcoholic. With no competent guidance in his life, he had no role model to guide him otherwise. His parents thought it was funny to put alcohol in his bottles, so by the time he was five he was an alcoholic.

During her hospital stay, my mother had asked that he not allow his 17-year-old nephew to be at the house while she was gone. As fate would have it, he stopped on the way home from dropping her off, picked him up and brought him home. There were days of coming in from school to find him naked lying on the couch. He would run around the house rubbing his privates in front of us, or rubbing his penis on my face telling me he knew I wanted it.

On this one late fall day, we got off the school bus and opened the door to home. Again, we found this teenaged boy naked on the couch waiting to taunt us. This day, however, was different because it changed my older brother's life and mine forever. After a little while, he walked over to me where I was sitting on the couch ignoring him. This particular day this boy did not stop at taunting, he picked me up and carried me to the back bedroom where my sister and I slept, closed the door and locked it behind him, and threw me on the bed. And so began one of the saddest days of my life.

My brother ran down the hall behind us trying to stop the door from closing. Being smaller and weaker than the young man my brother could not keep it open. He knew from being 14-years-old what was about to happen to me. He beat and kicked on that door until he was exhausted, and after a few minutes just slid to the floor outside that door screaming and crying for him not to hurt me. I can still hear his screams and the banging on that door, the helplessness in his voice because he could not help me. I was finally able to wiggle myself off the bed, out from under this jerk, and made my way to unlock the door. My brother and I never talked about what happened in that room. We went into the kitchen and began making dinner and waiting for our step dad to get home. I burned the rolls that night but we ate them anyway.

CHAPTER 4
I SAW THE LIGHT

I did not have many friends during my childhood so the few I did have were very special to me. When I was six years old, we were living in a small town in Alabama going to a school, which was miles away from home. Our home was located a ways back off a clay dirt road with neighbors spread over a long distance. Every morning and every afternoon, my brothers and sister would walk down this clay dirt road to the bus stop when the weather was pretty.

Two sisters who lived a few miles further down from our bus stop also rode this bus. They were mean and hateful sisters. Their life goal was to bully everyone on this bus and to make life as miserable as they humanly could. Every day I went to school, I would hate to get on the bus because they seemed to bully me the most out of all the kids on that stupid bus. One of the sisters was my age and could beat up any boy on this bus. Each day these sisters would get off at our bus stop and beat us up before we walked the road home.

DEBORAH UPTON

One day in particular I noticed things were different but did not understand at the time. The young bully who had beaten me up every day for months was different. She was being nice, singing songs, and not bothering me. It was a Friday afternoon and we were on our way home. Instead of being a bully she sat in her seat at the back of this bus singing a song that I had never heard before. As the bus drove on she continued singing, "I saw the light, I saw the light, no more of darkness, no more of night. Now I'm so happy, no trouble in sight, praise the Lord, I saw the light".

When we arrived at our stop, as usual, the sisters got off the bus. My only thought was that the songs were over and the fists would commence. But not this day! This day the strangest thing happened. The young bully asked me if I knew this Jesus man and I told her I had never heard of him. She told me that she was sorry for being so mean to me and that Jesus did not like it. She told me that she had never had a friend before and asked if I would be her friend. Excited to finally have a friend, I agreed that I would like to be hers. She and her older sister started for home.

Early Saturday morning the telephone rang and I could hear my mother talking about an accident on Friday night. After the girls had arrived home on Friday afternoon the oldest one, who was 16, wanted to go out on a date. Their parents were out of town and the only way she could go out was if their oldest sister, in her mid twenties, would come and take my friend and her baby sister, nine months old, to spend the night with her. She lived in the next town over. After picking up the girls and heading back towards town, she came upon a small country bridge. The truck in front of her dropped a rocking chair from its load in the back and the sister's car swerved, hitting the guardrail, and nose diving into the creek below.

The baby was thrown through the windshield and washed down stream. The driver was severed in half upon impact. My new friend who was a good swimmer was thrown out the passenger window and under the car. She was wearing a dress at the time which was caught under the front tire pinning her under. In the blink of an eye, all three girls were gone. My friend was gone forever and I was alone again.

I remember crying until I could not cry anymore. I was angry because for months I had not liked this girl because she was so mean, and now she was my new friend and died. Who was this Jesus person and why had He taken my new friend? Could He not find His own friends? I did not understand why He would want me to be alone. Why had this girl changed so much, and why on this day before?

CHAPTER 5
EARS BUT CANNOT HEAR

I t is the fourth grade and I am eight years old. I cannot tell you when it happened, only that it did. I at some point began having problems with my hearing and found it more difficult than usual to make out what people were saying. I could not say anything to my mother because money was already tight enough and I was not going to do anything that would get me in trouble. I seemed to be the child who was the most submissive, and yet found myself being in trouble more than anyone else. It seemed that no matter what I did it was never good enough.

Without my even knowing what I was doing, I had learned to read lips in school so that I would know what my teachers were saying. I moved to the front of the class when they worked on the chalkboards, and kept my eyes on them. My grades continued to be straight "A's" so no one knew but me.

It was a Saturday morning and I was helping my mother

to clean her room. I had my back to her so I could not hear when she spoke to me. My secret was out! This particular morning while dusting her dresser she had said something to me that I did not hear. Apparently she was screaming at me and I was being stubborn and ignoring her. Angered by my stubbornness she flew across the room and slapped me on the side of my head, which caught my attention.

Startled and crying I began trying to tell her I did not hear her, which only made her even angrier because I was not more than 10' from where she had been standing. When I continued screaming that I could not hear her she became so angry that she screamed that she would take me to the doctor and get my ears checked but that I had better hope the doctor found something wrong.

At the doctors office on Monday he continued his exam. When he got to my ears, he stopped, looked at my mother and asked how long I had been deaf. He told her that I had an inner ear infection that was so bad it had taken my hearing. He could not promise that when the infection was cleared I would regain my hearing.

This discovery astonished my teachers because I had had no problems in school. They looked at all the warning signs and I had not been causing trouble, my grades had not dropped, and I showed no signs or symptoms of being in any pain. The antibiotics cleared the infection and I eventually regained total hearing without any permanent damage.

CHAPTER 6
SIGNING FOR LOVE

The seventh grade was an interesting year for me. I was running from bullies, trying to survive an abusive home life, and wanting to die all at the same time. I was tired of being beaten until the blood blisters formed, tired of being beaten yet again because those blisters burst and splattered the wall, which made a mess I had to clean up, and did not find one thing in this world which interested me. I saw no purpose for being here and just wanted to die.

I had been a loner my whole life and this year was no different. With no friends and no one to talk to or share with I kept to myself. Everything I felt was bottled up and buried deep within me so that the outside world could not see. I had learned early in my childhood how to separate myself and to build walls to block out the things which I did not want to feel; hurt, pain, loneliness, and lifelessness. A lifetime spent dreaming and planning how I would kill myself if I ever saw the opportunity. After all no one would even know I was gone.

One day while sitting in my social studies class, the door opened, I could see across the hall into the classroom next door. What I saw interested me. It was a boy my age with his sister; she was doing something with her hands and it made me want to know more. I watched the two of them for a long time before class was over. Each day I would look forward to that class so that I could watch for more.

Much to my surprise, about a week later this girl said hello to me in the hall. She handed me a note and walked away. The note was from this boy telling me that he thought I was pretty and wanted to be my boyfriend. WOW! A boy thought I was pretty. I did not feel pretty but he said I was. Later that week his sister arranged for us to meet at lunch. I was excited because he was cute and thought I was pretty, but more than that, I would not be eating by myself.

The days went by with no word from him. I began to feel that he was involved in the ploy to tease me and was making it his duty to make me look stupid. Come on, this boy was cute, he could have any girl in the school, and he wanted me to be his girlfriend. Yeah, right! So I went about my merry way forgetting about him and convinced myself that I was stupid. I would not look at him if he passed, or talk to his sister because I did not want to be hurt anymore. I went back into my shell and hid.

Weeks went by like this until that glorious day when I discovered the real reason why he did not try to contact me. You see this boy had his own issues. It turned out that he had been born deaf and was afraid that I would laugh at him. Everyone in the school teased him about having to have his sister in class with him in order to do his work. The two of them had been taught sign language in order that they could communicate without disturbing others in the class.

After learning this, I asked his sister to teach me so that I could talk to him. We spent our recess time and any other moment we could steal so I could learn to communicate with the cute, blonde haired boy who liked me and thought I was pretty. He was astonished that I would want to learn to sign for him, or that I would want to be his girlfriend.

His family moved that summer and I never saw him or his sister again. In the late 70's while watching a band concert on television I received the surprise of my life. There to my amazement, on my television, was the cute blonde haired boy and his sister. There they were, now a famous brother and sister-singing duo, live on my television. I learned more about love from the two of them than I had learned from anyone else.

CHAPTER 7
HIGH SCHOOL WITHOUT THE HIGH

High school was more of the same for me; sadness, sexual abuse, and a violent alcoholic home. I did not dare find friends because I would not be able to go over to their house, and I certainly would not have been able to bring them home. Loneliness had become my favorite friend.

Night after night lying in bed wondering why I was alive. Thinking and dreaming of ways I could kill myself and end my misery as well as everyone else's. Lying in bed at night listening to the endless arguing, drunken tantrums, and the continuous beating of my mother was more than I could handle. I can remember feeling totally helpless and could see no way out.

Night after night, since the age of five, lying in my bed praying to a God I did not know about that He would send my daddy to rescue us. You see it was around this time that I had found one of those baby pillows which said where you were born and who your parents were that I discovered this evil alcoholic was not my father. I did not dare tell anyone I knew this information because that would mean more beatings for me. I had been snooping where I did not belong. Why had my mother married him? Why did she continue to subject her children to his torture? What was wrong with her?

Every night, begging and pleading that if this God was real, if He was as loving and merciful as I had heard He was then He would send my daddy to save us from this nightmare called life. Quietly screaming at Him that He did not love me like the Bible said He did, how could He. He was not as strong and loving of His children, after all, He was supposed to keep His children from harm, and He chose not to. He hated me as much as everyone else did and wanted me to suffer. At this point, I was angry with Him and hated hearing His name because He did not care either. I used to imagine Him sitting in this place called heaven laughing at me and making fun of how my life was hopeless and I was too stupid to do anything about it.

By the age of sixteen I found a job working as a receptionist in a credit union. I went to school all day and worked as much as I could to keep from going home. My life consisted of going to school, leaving there and going to work, leaving work and going home to help prepare dinner, wash the dishes, help the smaller ones with their homework and then secretly lying in bed with a flashlight to do mine, if I had not had time to do it before bedtime. I had to maintain that straight "A" average or I thought it would be hell for me. Sadly no matter how much I did it was never enough. I could always do better.

There was no time for friends or a social life. I did not date or attend any of the high school functions because I was too afraid to ask. My life consisted of graduating, turning eighteen, and moving out as fast as I could.

Graduation night finally arrived! Escorted by my parents I attended that ceremony and was more excited than I had ever been. In spite of my circumstances I made it. Our graduation song was one of greater significance to me than any of those graduates knew. Barry Manilow's "Looks like we made it" played over that speaker system and brought more heart felt joy to me than I could have imagined. At the end of the ceremony my step-father screamed that it was time to go home. I stood there as my classmates all celebrated and made their evening plans, and I had to go home, alone. Here I was a high school graduate with no money or hope of college and had no clue what life held for me. I had no hope of a prosperous future or living past today.

I left the job at the credit union and went to work as a purchasing secretary. For the first time I had a goal. I would work as hard as I could until I could save enough money to move out. As my life would have it, life had other plans. With money being tight and food needing to be bought, my mother started writing bad checks to the local grocery store. She had been hiding it from everyone because she knew it would mean serious consequences if my step-father found out. Then began the certified letters from law officials, if these checks were not paid she would be going to jail.

My older brother had been kicked out of the house months earlier so as the oldest of the remaining children it became my responsibility. Every penny I made, except for gas money, went to pay these checks off. They never seemed to stop coming. Paycheck after paycheck there would be more. I would never have the money to move out. My mother would tell me that I was not moving out because she needed me there to help her so to shut up talking stupid and face the facts. Months went by and I started seeing that my mother was right. I was too stupid to figure out how to get the money together to move out and finally be out of this life I had been thrown in to. I would die living in this violent home, not feeling like I belonged and not being loved.

CHAPTER 8
FEBRUARY 17, 1979

A t my wits end, I decided that today would be the day I would leave home despite what anyone else said or thought. I had spoken with my grandmother who was now living alone and she agreed to let me move in with her. I had spent all night on the 16th packing everything I could find, which was not much, into brown paper grocery bags and hiding them in the bottom of my closet.

I waited until my stepfather had left for work, helped with breakfast and cleaned the kitchen, then waited for my mother to busy herself with whatever she was doing. Quietly I walked into my bedroom and gather the first of the bags from the closet floor and headed for the back door. The first of the bags was in my car. As I eased back into the house my mother greeted me in the den and asked what I thought I was doing. I explained to her that I was going to live with my grandmother and that I needed to get out and try to make it on my own. I could not have imagined what happened next.

I started towards my bedroom to gather some more of my things. Reaching into the closet to pick up more grocery bags filled with clothes I lifted them up, turned to go out of the closet and was greeted by my mother. There she stood in the doorway of the closet, a 22 automatic pistol in her hand hammer cocked and pointed directly at me. The look on her face was one of pure lifelessness. She did not blink or move, she just stared at me, tears running down her face and hopelessness in her stare.

Moments went by before either of us spoke. I asked what she was doing and without hesitation she said "I will see you dead before I let you leave". I did not understand but knew at that moment that she meant what she was saying. There was no doubt that she was about to shoot me. Hugging those grocery bags close to my chest I slowly eased to the floor and sat down. If she was going to shoot me I would not watch her do it.

Just as I was preparing to die at the hands of my mother, the sound of my step-fathers truck startled her and she ran out of the room. One of the other kids had called him at work and told him that our mother was holding a gun to me and was going to shoot me. She ran into where she had gotten the pistol and placed it back in the drawer, walked into the den and started acting like nothing was wrong.

I grabbed everything I could put in my arms, decided that what I could not carry out with me would be left behind, and headed for the den and the back door. As I entered the den my mother who had been sitting on the couch, jumped up and taking her fist hit me on the side of the head knocking me to the floor. She continued hitting on me and screaming "you are not leaving". My step-father pulled her off me and threw her the couch. She got up running towards me swinging her fists. He again pulled her from me, threw her on the couch and sat on top of her screaming at me to get out. I ran as fast as my legs could go to my car and sped away.

I can remember getting to the freeway and driving as fast as I could towards my grandmother's house. The closer I got the more I talked to myself. I could not let her see me cry. She could not know what had happened because that was her daughter and I would be the one in trouble. I had to find a way to convince my grandmother that everything was good and that nothing had happened. She would never know.

Arriving at grandma's I had gathered up my strength and with a smile on my face I rang the doorbell. "I can do this", I kept telling myself. In what seemed like hours, the door slowly opened and there stood my grandmother, happy to see me and glad that I was moving in. She asked how I was doing. I opened my mouth to say "fine" and fell to the floor in hysterics. I can remember crying so hard that I could not breathe as I told her what my mother had just done. I tried to convince her that my mother knew where I was and would come and kill me I was not safe and could not stay there.

She walked to her room and came back with a pill which she called a Valium. Told me to take it and that we would leave for a while. She put me in her car and drove to the mall. She was determined to calm me down and make life matter. We had lunch, and shopped for a while before heading home. She was right, my mother did not come after me, and I was not going to die. For the first time I had found a place with no screaming, no fighting, and no beatings. The quiet peacefulness of that house overwhelmed me.

CHAPTER 9
UNCLE MATTHEW

Soon after moving in with grandma, both of us working and keeping to ourselves, the phone calls began. It was midnight, the house was quiet, all was well, and the telephone rang. It was the police department for my grandmother. They had picked a man up from an abandoned house who claimed to be her brother. We got up, dressed, and headed for town. It was my uncle Matthew, drunk, dirty and homeless. He had found shelter in an abandoned building downtown.

With much reluctance we took him home with us. With no place to put him, I gave him my bed and slept on the couch. Our goal was to clean him up, dry him out, and help him to find work. This was not the Uncle Matthew I knew. The one I knew was strong, had a beautiful home, a great job, a beautiful wife, and children. He had it all and I did not understand what went wrong.

Somewhere his life had gone wrong. He started

drinking and lost his job. Began spending time with other women and eventually lost his wife and children. Alone and with nothing left, he drank more and could not hold a job. Living any where he could find to live, grabbing meals where he could get them, and sleeping in any place he could find. What had happened to this man who once had it all? How could you go from having the dream life to having nothing?

With him bathed we tucked him in bed and spent the next week taking turns sitting with him at night cleaning up his vomit, watching him withdraw from the drugs and alcohol, and prayed that he would live through it. Weeks went by and finally, there stood in front of us, my uncle Matthew. Clean, shaven, and ready for the world again. We helped him to find a job and continued to give him a place to live until he could get on his feet.

Much to our surprise, the day came when Uncle Matthew did not come home from work. We waited and waited for him but he never showed up. Days went by and he never showed. We went to his job only to learn that he was not showing up there either. So for weeks we waited. Again, in the dead of night, the telephone rang. It was the police department again.

This telephone call was different. This time they had found the body of a man in an abandoned building. Apparently the man had been beaten and the building set on fire. He had been rushed to the county hospital with third degree burns all over his body. They had found a wallet on him that listed my grandmother's name as next of kin. We flew to the hospital to ID this man who was almost unrecognizable. With only a glimpse of his eyes we knew it was him.

We sat by his bedside until we were told he would survive and would be released to us to go home. Again, we took him home, gave him a bed, food, clothing, and all the love we could muster up. We hoped and prayed that this time would work. This time would be different because he would see the error of his ways and reform with our help. We spent weeks of treating burns, cleaning his vomit, bathing him, feeding him, and just loving him back to health.

Finally he was on his way to being able to find work and a place of his own. Finally all our hard work had paid off. He was stronger, healthier and happier than ever. He did find work and was doing great. He stayed sober, worked hard, and was very grateful for all we had done for him. He had hope for a future and looked forward to it. Again, the day came when he did not come home. Weeks went by with no phone calls, no letters, and no word of Uncle Matthew. Grandma and I would drive through town at all hours of the night looking for him. We called morgues, police stations, hospitals, but no word.

Six months went by when finally there was a telephone call from Uncle Matthew saying that he had met a woman and was happy. He was inviting my grandmother and me to his home to meet his new lady love. We made plans and did go to his home. Neither of us liked her and felt that she would not be good for him as she drank and we felt that he would find it harder to stay clean. He disagreed with us and asked us to leave. We did.

Weeks went by without a word. Eventually we received one last telephone call. It was the county morgue. They had found the body of a man earlier that night and wanted us to come and ID him and see if it was Uncle Matthew. It was. His woman friend had convinced him that he could drink and it would not hurt him. He lost his home, his job, and found himself back on the street.

This particular night he had run in to some others who

had been taking advantage of the homeless and that is where his life ended. After trying to fight them off and finding there were too many of them, he was overcome by their brutal force and passed out. They kicked him into a ditch; beaten, battered, with multiple broken bones, poured gasoline on his body and set him on fire. We made the arrangements and buried him. He was finally free.

CHAPTER 10
TOLEDO BEND

I had finally had enough. I was tired of being the good girl trying to do the right thing and finding myself alone and in despair. I had reached the end of my rope and did not care about anything anymore except trying to find the courage to end my miserable life. In all that I had survived to this point, the one thing I wanted the most was to die and did not seem to find the strength to do it myself. In a last ditch attempt I finally decided that I would have to live life dangerously until I found someone who would do it for me.

It was a Friday afternoon. I had gotten off work early, met up with a friend of mine (my only friend) and we started driving around. We found ourselves in a bad neighborhood which was not the place for two young "nice" girls to be. We were driving around trying to find some place to land when we saw a motorcycle shop. Having no place else to be we agreed that it would be fun to stop and look around. We were the ripe age of eighteen and did not have plans for the weekend.

We walked in this place and began flirting with every male we saw. We were both dressed to kill and flirting like we knew what we were doing. Finally one of the owners told us that a group of them had plans to go to Toledo Bend for the weekend and asked if we were interested. Why not, we had no other plans. We flew home, packed a small bag, threw on our shortest shorts and crop tops and met them back at the shop. Dressed for trouble, hair flying in the wind, we found ourselves on the back of bikes with people we did not even know, and did not care.

Some hours later we arrived in Toledo Bend with only our backpacks, and this group of couples who were longtime friends and carefree. We had not told anyone where we were going, so we were in this place with people we did not know, and no way home. I had left a note for my grandmother telling her I was out with my friend for the weekend and would be home on Sunday. Reality finally hit when they started settling in for the night. Who would sleep where and with whom? It was unanimously decided that we would all take the canoe over to an island in the middle of the lake and sleep there. Of course, my friend and I did not vote.

It is getting dark, we are on the island, no one knows where we are, and it is starting to occur to us both that we may have messed up here. The guys were starting to stir around, making these plans about the weekend, and who would have first shot at the fresh meat who had accompanied them. More than ever before, we knew that we had messed this one up and would now have to pay the price in order to get home safely. We both agreed that no matter what we had to do, we would play along with them until we could find ourselves safely back at her car. We were two young girls, alone with this gang, and had no one but ourselves to blame for the predicament we found ourselves in. We realized for the first time that our choices were about to suffer some dire consequences.

With nightfall getting closer and the two of us getting more scared by the minute I finally had a plan that might work. I asked my friend to trust me and to play along with what I said, even if it sounded utterly crazy. I had made a decision that would eventually keep the both of us safe. You see, my friend had never been with anyone and was in fear of losing her virginity to this group. I on the other hand, had not seen that part of me since the age of two and did not have anything to lose. It was what I felt I was born to be, a free ride for every man's pleasure.

I found the leader of this group and told him that my friend was very sick with some type of infection that the doctors could not cure. I went on to tell him that she had been living with this man who gave her this infection and the doctors told her she was going to die because they did not know what it was or how to cure it. The doctors told her that she could not be sexually active because she would give this infection to anyone she had sex with. I was lying my butt off but it seemed to be working. I told him they could do what they wished with me but to please leave my friend alone. He agreed.

The boys built a campfire and started laying out sleeping bags, one and then another. My heart raced inside me because I knew that I would not enjoy this weekend, but had to suffer my consequences. At least they all agreed to leave my friend alone. One by one they started coming up to me and pulling me towards them and towards where they had lain their sleeping bags. One by one I watched in horror as they started fighting over who would have me first.

With no place to run and hide I started trying to separate myself so that I would not feel what I knew was coming. I wanted to be as dead on the outside as I felt on the inside, and that is when it changed for me. With my friend safely tucked away in a sleeping bag next to the leader of this group I gave up any hope of surviving without recourse. Just then this leader stepped between me and the others. He announced that if anyone was going to have me, he was.

He went on to say that if any of the others touched me they would answer to him. Then he led me over to where he had set up camp for the night. He sat me down on a sleeping bag next to his (my friend was sleeping on the other side of him), and he said the most amazing words I had ever heard. For hours this man told me about himself, and what his life had taken him through. He then went on to tell me what he saw in me and how he felt that I had been through a similar experience. He explained to me that for the remainder of the weekend I would stay close to him and that he would protect me from the others.

He told me that no one there would touch me without my permission, and that he would see to it that my friend and I were safe. He tucked me into my own sleeping bag and brushed my hair until I fell asleep. The next morning he took me out to the edge of the island and asked me if I had ever fired a gun, at which time I told him I was afraid of guns. He spent all day teaching me about guns, how to handle them, how to load them, how to shoot them, and about gun safety. He explained that never again would I not be able to defend myself. How did he know so much about me when I had never said a word and my friend did not know? Why did this young man care about me and protect me when I had asked for it?

He kept his promise and my friend and I had a great weekend. For the first time ever, I laughed, sang songs, and enjoyed being alive. I did not understand but it was a nice change. On Sunday afternoon we left for home stopping only once to eat. I later learned that this group of bikers were well known and had reputations for being horrible people.

My friend and I never talked about that weekend again. We had so many unanswered questions and yet who would we ask. We knew that we had experienced something that was foreign to us but could not find the words to explain what had happened. Why were we spared? Why...Why...Why?

CHAPTER 11
LISTEN TO YOUR HEART

I t was a Friday afternoon, my friend and I had no plans for the weekend when I received a telephone call from my brother who is one year younger than me. He and a friend of his wanted the two of us to go to their high school dance with them, as they had no dates. We talked it over and decided that we had nothing to lose and it was plenty safe, so we arranged to meet them at my mother's house.

We arrived at the planned time and as I walked in the backdoor there sat in the recliner my brother's friend. He stood 6'2" weighing 175 pounds; broad shouldered, and looked really cute. I was impressed by his looks, but my heart was telling me to turn the other way, that this was not the one chosen for me. What did my heart know? It was just a dance! Introductions were made and we left for the dance. I loved to dance but this boy did not. He did not know how. I told him I would teach him but he did not want to.

Eventually I became tired of standing around and told

him that if he was not going to dance with me I would find others to dance with, and that is exactly what I did. Two years earlier I had graduated from this same school and knew the faculty. I danced with teachers, school counselors, and other students I did not know. I was in the safety of my brother and had no fear. The slow songs I would dance with my brother's friend if he wanted to.

Arriving back at home this boy said the funniest thing. He explained to me that he had told my mother weeks earlier, after seeing my graduation picture hanging on her wall, that he would marry me someday, and that I would be the mother of his children. He went on to say how you take a girl out, buy her a coke, and cannot even get a kiss goodnight. I looked dead at him, told him he was a baby who needed to go home to his mommy, and went inside.

He called the next day and asked me to a movie; again my heart told me to leave this one alone, and again I ignored it. No harm was going to happen. He was just a lonely boy, who had found an older girl, would that not impress his friends! For weeks he called and asked and each time I would call my brother and invite him. Within weeks this boy gave me a card which said that he wanted to marry me someday and that he hoped our children turned out just like me.

At Thanksgiving I finally met his family. I had just had major surgery and was not getting around too good. This young man had picked me up from the hospital earlier that morning. His mother did not approve of me because I was older than him by eleven months. She called me "an older woman of the world" who was out to corrupt her son. She wanted me to leave her son alone and stay away from him. She told me that I was not good enough for her son and I certainly would never be the mother of her grandchildren. She liked another girl that he had dated and wanted them to get back together. His dad was a kind man who treated me like one of the family.

Five months passed from our meeting and his mother took ill. She was in need of major surgery to save her life. I visited her in the hospital every day. Surgery went well but left her very weak and in great pain. I spent days in that hospital room helping her to eat, holding her up, while standing her in the shower, to bathe her. Still I was not good enough for her son.

Eventually she asked if I would move into her house and take care of her boys (her two sons and her husband) until she could get home and get on her feet. I agreed to but not without recourse. I told them that I would not have the neighbors thinking that I was living with someone I was not married to. The next day we woke early, went to my doctor's office for the appropriate blood work, which was required back then, went to get our license, and was married in the office of the pastor where my mother attended church that afternoon.

We left the church; I dropped him off at work and went home. Later that evening we went to the hospital to tell his mother. She was furious! How dare I trap her son in a marriage she did not want! She forbids him to go on a honeymoon (we were going to Galveston for the weekend) and we left. Instead of celebrating our marriage he invited a friend of his and his friend's sister (an old girlfriend) to go with us to the destruction derby that was in town.

At home, he was getting showered and changed to leave, his friends in the living room waiting. It is my wedding night and this girl proceeds to go into the bathroom to watch him shave and dress. I became angry and they laughed because to them it was funny. One would have thought that would have been my first clue.

My next clue came later that night when we were home

alone. I had not dealt with any of the baggage from my past. Excited to be married because now there was someone in my life that "had" to love me, he had no choice, he was my husband and a husband is supposed to love his wife. The one thing I did not figure in to this equation was the "wifely" duties. Here I was now, married and had a responsibility to my husband. I did not dare tell him about my past; after all, I was told that if I said anything to anyone they would not love me.

I buried myself deep within me and decided that I would make any sacrifice to be loved. I wanted children and to the best of my knowledge that was the only way to get them. We immediately began trying to have a baby. Months went by with no success so I started going to fertility specialists. It was during this time that I discovered that all the abuse from my childhood had left irreversible damage to my insides. I would probably never conceive a child of my own. I had surgery after surgery with no success.

With the help of massive fertility drugs I finally conceived. One night we were lying in bed, my husband and I were asleep and the house was quiet. Four months pregnant, I was awakened by a feeling of someone being in the room with us. When I opened my eyes, there at the foot of the bed stood my grandfather, who had been dead for years. He immediately started saying, "Debbie Do, do not be afraid. You have to be careful now or you will lose her". Then he vanished. I thought I was crazy and never said a word to anyone. The next day I started bleeding, was placed on bedrest, and five months later gave birth to a beautiful baby girl.

CHAPTER 12
ALLIGATOR TEARS

T hings made a dramatic change for me after my daughter's birth. Here I had this beautiful baby that I could love, and who would love me back, and yet something deep inside me had begun to change. I felt overwhelmed with all the new responsibilities, and smothered by this feeling of sadness. My husband's world seemed to revolve around this baby and there was nothing left for me. All his free time was spent with her. We did not talk anymore, we did not go out alone anymore, and it was all about her. I knew that I loved my baby girl with my life, but I began to resent my husband for forgetting about me.

By the time she was a year old I had developed female cancer from all the damage to my insides (scar tissue from rips and tears). The doctors wanted to do surgery but I wanted more children. I began chemotherapy and prayed that it would work. It eventually went in to remission and I began the regimen of going in for biopsies every six months. In going to all the specialists I soon discovered what had caused it. All the abuse from my childhood, and the depression had stunted my pituitary glands causing the natural growth hormones to cease. The damage was irreversible and my body did not produce the normal hormones that women's bodies make.

My husband became tired of my being sick and moody all the time so he started working more and staying out all night. When he was home he was playing with the baby and ignoring me, or we were fighting. This left me with a baby to tend to by myself and a total feeling of helplessness. I became very suicidal. He did not love me, my baby did not love me, and I was not a good wife or mother. I hated me and I hated the world for making me.

Months went by like this. I had started noticing that when my husband was home, our daughter would go and sit in the bottom of her closet and close the door. I knew this was not normal behavior for a baby and tried to talk to him about it, but he kept telling me it was my fault. He kept telling me, "Look at that, your own baby does not want to be around you." At the end of my rope, I could not take anymore. I knew that I had to die in order to spare her any more pain.

It was mid-morning, early in the spring, and I had never felt more hopeless than I did at that time. I had lost down to 89 pounds and was deeply depressed. After yet another fight with my husband, he told me he was divorcing me and taking my daughter because I was unfit and did not deserve her. I knew I had to do something so I went into the kitchen, grabbed a bottle of pills and proceeded to get me a glass of water. He heard the pill bottle rattle and ran into the kitchen. When he saw what I was doing he grabbed the back of my neck, poured that bottle of pills into my mouth, and screamed at me to swallow them, and went back to the bedroom to pack.

For the first time I became angry. I spit those pills into the sink, reached up into the cabinet and pulled out the 22 caliber automatic pistol that we kept there. I began trying to load the clip when he heard me and came running. He grabbed the gun from my hand and I started grabbing hands full of bullets and putting them in my pockets. For what I did not know, it was not as if I could use them. At that moment all I knew was that I wanted him dead, and if I had to bite those bullets to shoot him I would.

At that moment I heard the tiniest, sweetest little voice from behind. My daughter had heard the commotion and come from her room to see. I spun around to find this beautiful little girl, which I loved more than my own life, standing there with alligator sized tears running down her face. The only words coming from her mouth were "I will be a good girl now mommy, I will be a good girl, please do not be mad". What had I done to my baby?

I immediately fell to my knees and grabbed her in my arms. I hugged that baby like I had never hugged her before. I told her that she was a very good girl and that mommy was not mad at her; such a small angel with so much power. I set her down and grabbed the phone book. I knew that I needed help and could not do this alone. I called every psychiatrist in that book, explained to each of their secretaries what the problem was, and begged for help. Each one telling me that it was lunchtime and I would need to call back after lunch and make an appointment.

I had one last call to make before I had made them all. The phone rang and the receptionist answered. I explained to her that I needed help and I needed to see the doctor because my husband hated me, I hated me, but more so my baby girl hated me. I just kept telling her that I had called everybody else and no one would help me. She asked me if I could hold while she talked to the doctor who was on his way out to lunch and I agreed. A few minutes later she came back and asked how long it would take me to get there, that he would wait on me. I grabbed my purse and flew.

Driving to this office I convinced myself that I would not cry and that he would not find anything wrong with me. I walked in, filled out the paperwork, and sat down in his office. He asked how I was doing and that is when I lost any control I had ever had. I told him everything that had gone on. I wanted him to help me to die so that the people in my life would never be hurt by me again. I could not do that to my daughter she deserved a better mother. He explained that he wanted me to go to the hospital for a few days and let him run some tests. I explained that I needed to go home and do some things first and would think about it.

When I arrived back at home the house was quiet. There was no sign of my husband or daughter. I walked into our bedroom and found that everything had been taken except the bed. I went to my daughter's room and found it empty. This man had cleaned out that house and left while I was out getting help for myself so that I could be a better person. I walked into the living room, sat down on the couch to try and figure out what I was going to do. Figured I would watch some television while I sat there. I reached for the remote control and turned it on, only to find that it did not come on. I walked towards it to find out if it was unplugged and discovered that it was gone. He had taken everything.

I had two choices at this point, I could go to his mother's house where I knew he was and get my baby, or I could pack my bags and check myself into that hospital. I chose to pack a bag and drove to that hospital as fast as I could drive. I remember driving there, walking in the front door and begging the nurse to help me, but I did not remember anything else. Four days later I awoke in a hospital bed, did not know where I was or how I had gotten there. I was still wearing my clothes. I asked to go home. They called the doctor who came to talk to me about why I was there. He explained that I had checked myself in so I was free to check myself out. He also explained to me that he felt he could help me if I would give him the chance and that we could figure out through his tests why I was in my present state and he would help me to live a better more normal life.

I wanted to see my baby girl. I called my husband and asked him to bring her to see me and he refused. I begged him and finally the doctor called him and asked for him to come in to talk to him. He wanted to find out where my husbands intentions were on staying married or divorcing. He did eventually bring her in for an hour. The next day he came back for our joint meeting with the doctor.

During this meeting my husband told the doctor he wanted a divorce. He said that he was going to take my daughter away from me as I was unfit to raise her. The doctor told him that he could not prove me unfit and that he would spend his time preparing me for divorce and would see him in court on my behalf. He agreed that I was ill but that the courts would not remove my daughter from me, and that he would show the courts that I had admitted the problem existed and was, of my own free will, receiving help for those problems.

Six weeks I spent in that hospital working on myself and working towards a life of raising my daughter alone. All the tests and counseling sessions revealed a deep depression due to the variety of childhood abuse and a severe lack of naturally produced hormone. I was placed on hormone therapy and a regimen of anti-depressants; spent time learning to meditate and was released to home and joined the Adult Children of Alcoholics group. I drove myself home, called my husband and told him he could either bring my daughter to me or I would gladly go to his mother's house and get her. He brought her home. Weeks later, with half his things at home and half at his mother's house, I told him he needed to decide. He was either going to his mother's and bring the rest of his things home, or he could pack up what was there and leave; he could not live in both places and I needed a commitment from him one way or the other. He chose to stay.

CHAPTER 13
FIELD OF CONFUSION

W hile on our way to Hot Springs, Arkansas, to get away for a couple of days, the craziest thing happened, as if my life had not already been crazy enough. My husband was driving along watching the road; I was staring out the window, my mind going all sorts of places. How much effort would it take to open the truck door and jump to my death? How much pain would I feel if the tires were to run over me? How would I ensure that if I jumped at just the right timing the car in the other lane would run over me? Would I die or would I be left a mangled mess, alone and unattended? These were just a few of the things playing over and over in my head.

For hours I stared out that window thinking very crazy thoughts. The roadside was the same; dried, dead grass which was overgrown and needed water and mowing. We were now in Arkansas headed to Hot Springs. I was still staring out the side window thinking of ways to die without feeling any pain, when I saw the most amazing place.

One minute I was overly depressed looking at dried, dead grass, and the next I was looking at the most magnificent meadow I had ever seen. Acres and acres of the most luscious green grass; this was not your normal green, it was a deep indescribable color. I had never seen such green. Huge trees filled with large leaves, and acres and acres of flowers. There were yellows, purples, blues, reds, pinks, whites, and all kinds of colors. Deep beautiful colors, each one more yellow and more purple than I could ever explain to anyone.

I can remember the calmness and peace that I felt when I was looking at this place. The birds were flying around, singing as they went. In the middle of this meadow was a very large fountain of the most crystal clear water, and a brook that flowed straight down the middle of the field. I could almost hear the water running.

After what seemed like hours, I heard a truck honk his horn and turned to see what it was. It was nothing more than someone acting stupid so I immediately looked back around to the meadow beside me. Turning back I began to cry because that beautiful meadow that I had just been looking at was now overgrown, dead and dried grass that needed to be mowed. I looked behind me and saw nothing different.

What was wrong with me and why had I seen such beauty as I had never seen before if it was not there. I cannot explain what it was and have not seen it since, but it was there and I did see it.

CHAPTER 14
THE BATTLE CONTINUES

Despite counseling and the years of therapy my battles with depression continued. Those around me could not understand me or chose not to. I continued to feel alone, misunderstood, and unloved. I took parenting classes in order to become a better parent to my daughter. I was determined that her life would be better than my own, and that my internal battles would not affect her. She was going to have a better life if it killed me. I spent hours sitting in the floor playing with her, teaching her things, and making sure she knew that she was loved and accepted. Still locked in an unhappy marriage I centered my world around hers. I had failed as a human being but I would not fail as a mother.

When my daughter was two I began trying to conceive again. I was convinced that no man, including my husband, would love me if I could not give him a son. Time and time again I tried and each attempt failed. I went through surgeries and procedures which could have killed me, but I continued to try. After the final surgical procedure at one of the leading medical facilities in the country, it was determined that I was barren. That my insides had never reached maturity, and that I would need to go back to the same adoption agency where I had adopted my daughter. I laughed at the doctors and told them I had given birth to her. Their tests revealed that to be a medical impossibility. I had the insides of a pre-pubescent adolescent. There were no eggs in my ovaries, and my uterus had never given birth. It had been damaged early in my childhood and was nothing but scar tissue and unable to conceive much less carry a child to term. My husband told me that he did not need a son. He had his daughter and did not need anymore children.

I did eventually conceive with the help of massive doses of fertility drugs. Now I just needed to pray he was a son or that would be a definite guarantee that my husband would divorce me. Why would he stay with a woman who could not give him a son? Eight weeks into the pregnancy I began having complications and was placed on medication and bedrest for the remainder of my pregnancy. This placed even more strain on my marriage and our family. Our daughter was five at the time and having to learn to help with the things that mommy used to do because now this "stupid baby" was making her sick. I did eventually give birth to a healthy baby boy and thought life would begin to turn around for me and my family.

At three weeks of age, my beautiful baby boy began having these unexplainable spells. He was breastfed and would be eating when all of a sudden he would turn purple and go completely limp. Our daughter had done this at the exact same age. After admitting her to Children's Hospital it was determined that she had an ear infection which had poisoned her blood. When the blood would flow through her heart it would stop causing the symptoms.

I took our son to the same pediatrician as my daughter so he was aware of her condition. He immediately transferred him to Children's Hospital because his symptoms were much worse than our daughters had been. It was learned that he had a deficiency of the immune system in which the gene that controls the immune system was deformed. With this deformity, the bone marrow normally produces the good cells which combat infections; his bone marrow was producing more of the bad cells which were destroying the good ones as they were produced.

Because he had no immune system he was quarantined to the house. He could not go outside, be around anyone who was sick or even sneezing, the house had to stay sterile, and he was failing fast. In addition to all the medications he was eventually placed on a breathing machine to help with his lungs. At two months of age, our daughter brought chickenpox home from kindergarten. The doctor said not to worry as he had never heard of a two month old ever getting chickenpox. Wrong! He developed a worse case than his sister had had. Each one of those blisters turned blood red and developed a black ring around them. He was allergic to chickenpox. The doctor spent hours draining those things and placing medication on each one. We had to drain the poison from them as they developed to keep him from dying. A normal childhood disease was fatal to this little boy who looked so healthy.

By the time this baby was five months old I was on the phone to my psychiatrist making an appointment. I walked into his office, sat down, and was asked two questions. Boy or girl? How old is it? He immediately called my gynecologist and explained that I needed to be sterilized as soon as I could wean my son. He went on to tell him that because my body did not produce natural hormones that while I was pregnant my body overproduced those hormones and then after childbirth they bottomed out causing me problems with my chemical levels. I was advised not to have any more children because my hormones and chemistries would continue to bottom with each one. He went on to explain that my issues went way beyond postpartum depression.

I was sterilized and went home to continue trying to be everything that everyone else needed me to be. I was trying to tend to a baby who was critically ill and needed around the clock care, trying to stay involved in my daughter's school and be room mother and volunteer, as well as, Girl Scout leader and mother to all the neighbors kids who were latchkey kids. One might ask where my husband was during all this. He was either gone, asleep or out doing what he wanted to do.

At the age of eight months, my son was hospitalized to have his ears drained and tubes installed. It was discovered that due to all the fluid behind his ears, he was deaf. A simple procedure; a simple result. Not my son! It started out that way, but the end result was much more complex. It was decided that because of the weakness of his lungs, he would be given a shot of Valium and I would rock him until he fell asleep. They would then come in and get him to take him to surgery.

After a short time of rocking he fell asleep. The anesthesiologist came in to get him and his head popped up. He was wide awake and not leaving his mommy. They decided that due to time constraints they needed to take him on. Throughout his eight months he had endured blood tests every three days so he was not afraid of needles, and did not cry when they stuck him. They continued to administer the anesthesia but he did not respond. They increased the dosages and still he was looking around. They could not give him anymore without overdosing him so they decided to use a little gas. As soon as the gas was administered he began to fall asleep. Seconds later his heart stopped beating, his respiration and pressures dropped to zero. He was dead with slow brain waves.

They immediately began procedures to bring him back and were successful. As his tiny little life would have it, he was allergic to anesthesia. Now an operating room was faced with the greatest challenge of their careers. If they did not drain the fluid from his ears, he would die, if they tried to do the surgery he would die because they could not put him to sleep. It was decided that they had no choice but to continue. They increased the surgical staff and after getting him stabilized continued his surgery. Awake, alert and not crying, the doctors said they had never seen anything like it.

The next three years were even more difficult for me. Now with his hearing, he was extremely sensitive to any noise. The slightest sound would have this child screaming in terror. Still quarantined from the world, I was a prisoner in my own home and feeling more alone than ever. Then the latest blood work sent my world spinning. He showed the signs of leukemia. What else could go wrong? He needed a blood transfusion to build his immune system but none of us could be the donors. It seemed that his defected immune system was caused by one or both parents having the defected gene. We were all tested and it was discovered that we each had the defect.

At my wits end, yet again, I made a doctors appointment for myself. As I started explaining what I had been dealing with, and that I needed help for my son, the doctor started crying and asked me how I was holding up. I told him I was fine but needed help for my son. He immediately explained that if I could remain so calm as I explained my sons leukemia to him without a tear in my eye, I needed to be treated for depression. I was not depressed! I was tired of four years of not sleeping more than an hour a day, dealing with doctors on top of doctors, trying to be a good mother to my daughter, and trying to be everything that everyone else needed me to be. Who was I fooling?

I remember the day this beautiful little boy was standing in the front door watching his sister and her friends play in the front yard. We had put up a glass door so he could look out. Some of her friends started laughing at his bald head and calling him "baldy, no hair, sick boy…" For the first time my husband showed some compassion. He went into the bathroom and shaved his head so he could be like our son. He told all those boys in the front yard how cool it was to be bald and that our son was very sick and might die so they did not need to laugh at him. He told them they were lucky because they could play outside but that he could not. He asked them how they would feel if they could not go outside.

Finally, all is well. The medications decreased. The breathing treatments were discontinued, and we wait. Everything was going great and we were going to try to see if he would be able to go to public school. Kindergarten he missed more days than he went. It was excused so he graduated to first. Same for first grade missed more than he went. Second grade he became ill and had to be hospitalized again. His appendix had inflamed but due to his history of being allergic to anesthesia they could not operate. He spent a week in the hospital being fed massive doses of antibiotics to cool it down.

A child I was told I could never conceive, never carry to term, and would not live to be one year old, and then two, then…He graduated from High School last spring and is now attending college to earn his degree in Computer Networking and Securities.

CHAPTER 15
JOURNEY OF A LIFETIME

April 1997 began the battle of my life. I had gone to the doctor for a regular checkup and when the tests came back it showed a few abnormal cervical cells. I was called back to see the doctor three weeks later for a biopsy, which came back to show that these cells were rapidly advancing and the pathologist had placed a note on the report that this patient needed immediate surgery to remove the cervix and uterus. My doctor disagreed and wanted more tests. I spent the next three months going to urologists', psychiatrists, and other opinions. Finally going to a second opinion in July, my doctor had chosen one of his colleagues for the second opinion.

After the exam, and without taking any tests, he asked me to meet him back in his office. When I arrived in the office he asked if my doctor had done a pelvic, at which time I told him no, so he picked up his phone and called him. He told him that he needed to get me into surgery as soon as possible. He continued by telling him that if he had done a pelvic he would have felt the numerous masses which were now growing. I was scheduled for surgery the following week.

The cancer had advanced so rapidly that it consumed the entire pelvic cavity. The uterus and ovaries were all removed. The bladder and intestines had to be cleared of tumors and masses which had attached themselves to these organs. Surgery was successful and three days later I was released with a clean bill of health. For the first time ever I was free of pain.

Everything was going great. Three weeks after surgery I became ill. It was the first day of school for the kids and I had never missed taking them. This time I was vomiting profusely and could not sit up much less drive, so I asked a neighbor to take them. For days I continued vomiting with no relief. On the third day I called the gynecologist who politely told me it sounded like a viral infection to him and to call the family doctor. I called the family doctor who told me I needed to call my gynecologist because he had just done the surgery.

On the fourth day my husband came in from work to find me lying with my head in a trash can because I was too weak to move. He called the family doctor and told him I needed to be seen. He was told to have me in the office the next morning. Arriving at the doctors office I could not walk so they took me straight back to a room. The nurse went to tell the doctor that he needed to see me immediately because she did not think I looked very good. He came in, took one look at me and called for the hospital to come get me for admission.

Test revealed that during surgery when the tumors were being removed from my intestines, one had broken loose and was not removed. It had lodged in the small bowel and blocked the bowel. The lungs were filled with bile, my stomach was burned and the esophagus was covered in bleeding ulcers. They wanted to do more surgery to remove the blockage. I was lying in a bed with tubes in my nose, down my throat, and in my neck, draining bile as fast as possible and feeding me. I cannot hold my head up and they want to cut me again?

I told the doctor I would not consent to surgery because I did not feel I was strong enough to survive it and would die if he cut me again. I was told that they would have to cut me from the ribs down and open me completely up to repair the damage. I refused. I told him that I did not believe that God wanted me to be cut again and that He would heal me. My doctor disagreed and started the process to get a court order to do surgery. I asked for a phone and told him that if he would give me until 6:30 p.m. I would sign for it myself if God had not healed me. It was 5:30 p.m.

I called a friend of mine, a 70-year-old woman who had been my mentor for years, and asked her to have her Bible study class pray for me. I told her that I did not feel God wanted me to be cut on again so soon and that if they did this surgery I would die. I hung up the phone and told the doctor to wait the one hour; he agreed. That is when the journey began.

Not knowing what else to do, knowing that I knew that I knew I would die if they cut me open, I lay both arms beside me on that bed. I remember placing my arms, palms up, beside me and saying to myself, "Lord I do not believe that it is Your Will that I am cut open again. You are a merciful God who knows all things and can do all things. I trust You now to remove this blockage from my abdomen and to shine Your mercy down upon me. If it be Your Will that I go through this surgery then so it is written and so it shall be done, take care of my children. Thy Will be done Lord."

The next thing I remember was being in the whitest light I could ever imagine. I was surrounded by this magnificent light and feeling so peaceful and content. I kept thinking to myself that I did not want to leave this place. Then I realized that someone was speaking to me. This strong masculine voice kept saying the same thing repeatedly, "You have been chosen by Me, it is not yet your time." I was begging this voice not to send me back and it would repeat the same thing, "You have been chosen by Me, it is not yet your time."

Instantly I was back in my bed and one of the doctors was straddling me beating on my chest screaming for me to come back. When I opened my eyes I was surrounded by five doctors and some nurses with puzzled looks on their faces, just standing there staring at me. Finally my doctor walked over to the bed, sat down and picked up my hand in his, and asked me who I was. I told him "I am a nobody from a little town called ------, Georgia." He said, "you are anything but a nobody, where were you".

He continued by telling me that he did not know where I was but that God was right over there, we saw Him he kept saying as he pointed over to the corner of the room. He said that I had had a mild heart attack and a light stroke and they had hell bringing me back. But out of no where the corner of the room lit up and they saw God standing there. Then I came back. Who was I and where was I from? I answered them by telling them the same thing, "I am a nobody from a little town called -----, Georgia". Then I told them to go get there machine and check my abdomen because the blockage was gone. They did and it was.

For days I lay in that bed with nurses and doctors' coming to my room to see this wonder that everyone was talking about. They all wanted to visit this room. The only thing I knew was that I did not know where I had been but I liked it. I did not want to come back and if it was God's presence then He did not want me either. How many people could say they had been kicked out of heaven? I was angry. How bad did you have to be that God did not want you?

CHAPTER 16
THE CRASHING OF A WORLD

After returning home from the hospital I became obsessed with finding answers. I wanted to know where I had been, and why I was sent back to this place I referred to as hell on earth. I believed that I had been kicked out of heaven and that God did not want me either, and I wanted answers. But I also knew that I was overwhelmed with the need to tell everyone what I had seen and about this beautiful place we all had to look forward to.

I began looking for Bible studies to go to, reading my Bible, and studying workbooks on how to pray the correct way so that you receive answers back. I read book after book on life after death and hearing from God. I wanted to know what had happened to me. What friends I did have stopped talking to me because they thought I was crazy. My husband started staying gone all the time because he did not want to hear it either. I talked to my pastor who told me that I could not have seen anything like I had explained because it was impossible.

It was around this time I noticed that my home life was changing. With my husband gone all the time, supposedly working, I was alone most of the time. I would spend night after night sitting by the phone waiting to hear from him with nothing. No phone calls, no messages, and no idea where he was spending his time. I began studying on the subject of being a submissive wife. I felt that if I could be the wife God intended for me to be it would change things.

Soon my husband started coming home long enough to shower, dress and go out "to blow off steam". I did not like it but kept quiet. After a few days I came to the conclusion that if he was going out he would do it with honor. I believed that I was a reflexion of him and that if he looked good then to the outside world they would see he had a good wife at home who took care of him. So, every night I would starch and iron his clothes while he showered. When he became tired of wearing jeans, I went with him to pick out dress clothes.

Each night I would sit for hours waiting for a call that he was safe. I would call him but he would not answer the phone or return a message. When he would finally get home in the early hours of the morning I would have a hot meal on the table waiting for him. I sat for hours massaging his feet, legs and back, telling him how much I appreciated how hard he worked for his family. That he deserved some time out to unwind.

It became night after night sleeping with a man who was pulling further and further away from me. If I slept in the bed he would sleep on the floor, when he was home. Intimacy between us became nonexistent.

I knew that we were in trouble and asked him to please go to counseling with me. I begged him not to throw 23 years of marriage away. Desperate to save my marriage I knew that I had to make changes. I would go out and buy lingerie that I was embarrassed to wear and he would turn away from me. I would get in the shower with him and bathe him when he was too tired to bathe himself and he would turn away from me or push me away.

December 26th, 2002 was a day I will never forget. At my wits end on what to do about my marriage I did the one thing I had never done before. While he showered I retrieved his wallet from his pocket and shattered my world. In that wallet I found a receipt from a jewelry store where he had purchased a pair of diamond and black opal earrings on Christmas Eve; I did not receive them. The receipt was from a large jeweler which printed the name of the customer on the receipt, so his name was bold and clear.

When he exited the bathroom I was standing in the bedroom, receipt in hand. I asked him what it was and he denied ever seeing it. I went on to explain what it was and that his name was on it. He denied it and said it was not his. I became angry and screamed that his name was on it and that since I did not get the earrings where were they. He explained that I did not want his answer or what he had to say to me.

He sat down on the corner of the bed and started getting dressed in the clothes I had just starched and ironed. I backed up against the wall in front of him and slid to the floor begging him to talk to me. This man that I had given my soul to for 23 years said words to me that still today ring in my ears. He looked me dead in the face and said that he bought them for me but returned them because he did not want me to get my hopes up. I asked for the receipt and he told me he did not have a return receipt; they did not give him one. He then looked me dead in the face and continued telling me that he did not love me and that he was moving out and taking our son, now fifteen, with him.

He went on to say that I was not fit to breathe the same air as him, that I was unfit as a mother, that my children hated me, and that he could not get away from me fast enough. If that was not harsh enough he went on to scream at me, "Look at you Deborah Lynn. What man in his right mind would want that? The sight of you makes me sick and the sound of your voice makes me want to throw up." He stood up, walked out of the bedroom and left for the night.

Sometime during the early morning I fell asleep. At five in the morning on December 27th I woke up to an empty house. I ran to my sons' room to find it empty. I called my husbands phone and got his voicemail where I left a message for him to please call me back. A few minutes later my son called and fed my heartache even more. He told me that he did not want to live with me anymore and would be moving out with his dad. He told me not to call them anymore because he did not want to talk to me again.

My world to this point had consisted of two things, my husband and my children. I had given everything I had to them and kept nothing for myself. My daughter was married and living her life and now my husband and son hated me, I had nothing left. For the first time I realized that I had absolutely nothing left to live for and did not care if death hurt. In desperation, I called for over two hours to get them to answer the phone and work this out but they would not.

Finally with nothing else to lose I did the only thing I knew I could do. I picked up my Bible, a 22 caliber pistol, a fifth of Jack Daniels and walked into the bathroom. I lay the open Bible on my lap, broke the seal on the Jack Daniels and opened the bottle. Then I lay the pistol on the floor beside me. The agony of my pain was unbearable so I began crying and begging God to show me in the Bible that He would forgive me for what I was about to do.

For hours I searched for anything that would tell me that He would forgive me as I drank that whiskey. I sat screaming for God to please help me to find something; anything. I knew that it was not going to happen but I wanted Him to change something just for me. Eventually I realized that it was not going to happen so I decided on another plan. If I went to sleep and never woke up it would not be suicide.

I walked into the kitchen and grabbed a bottle of Vicodin. I had shattered my ankle a few days before and it was given to me for pain. I sat down in the kitchen floor, Jack in hand and swallowed 32 of those pills. Then I decided that it might not be enough so I grabbed a packet of Benadryl from the cabinet and swallowed approximately 30 of those, finished off the bottle of whiskey and took my Bible to bed with me.

At 3 a.m. on the 28th I woke up in a strange place. I sat up in the bed and gathered my bearings to discover that I was in my daughters' spare bedroom. With no idea how I had gotten there I walked outside and started down the street. I walked for a while, remembered what had happened the day before, and became very angry. Hell, I could not even kill myself right! I walked the streets until daybreak becoming even angrier.

When I felt she and her husband were awake I returned to the house with a vengeance. I wanted to know how I ended up there and why. I started cooking breakfast for them and trying to figure out what my next step would be once I received those answers. Apparently after I lay down my neighbor called to talk to me and I answered the phone. She did not like the way I sounded over the phone so she and her husband came to see about me. When they arrived they found the front door open and me unconscious on the bed hugging my Bible. The empty bottles lying on the kitchen floor so they became even more concerned and called my daughter.

They continued to sit with me until my daughter and her husband arrived. She did not want her dad, brother or anyone else to see me like that so she and her husband loaded me in their truck and took me home with them. We ate breakfast, I washed the dishes, and told them it was time for me to go home and fight for what belonged to me; my husband and my son.

I arrived home to an empty house and started cleaning. I called my husbands' phone and left a message that I was home and was not going anywhere. He called me back and was angry and told me to leave. I was angry and ready to fight so I proceeded to tell him he would have to kill me to get me out and hung up. He called several times and I did not answer the phone. I cleaned the floors, the walls, and everything else I could find to clean.

Determined to save my family I used my anger to lead me, after all I was born surviving and obviously God did not want me. I was stronger than I had been in months and ready for battle, or so I thought. I went to the bathroom, sat down on the toilet and discovered there was no toilet paper. Of all the things that were going on during that time, I lost it over a roll of toilet paper. There was none to be had in the house. My vehicle had been repossessed a week earlier due to nonpayment so I had no way to go get any, even if I had had money to pay for it.

About this time a friend of mine called and I started crying and told her that I had no toilet paper and no way to get any. Concerned about the way I sounded she came over and brought me a four pack and a pack of cigarettes. How stupid I must have looked over toilet paper! I had started attending college class's months earlier and took one roll and hid it in my backpack. That man would not leave me without again.

I buried myself in school and decided that I had to get my degree before my husband made any moves so that I could find work. I had been a stay-at-home wife and mother and had not worked since my daughter was born. In March of 2003, my daughter who was three months pregnant started having complications. I took her to a doctors' appointment for an ultrasound and saw the most precious baby I had ever seen in my life. My baby was having her first baby.

I was excited to become a grandmother but concerned about my daughter. A few days later I received a call from her saying she needed a ride to the doctor because she thought something was wrong. My husband and I headed over to her house and five minutes away she called me back to tell me that she thought she had just lost it and had called the doctor who wanted to see her.

When we arrived at her house she greeted me at the door to tell me that there was something in the bathroom that she wanted me to look at and that she needed me to take her to the doctor. We picked the baby up, placed it in a paper towel and Ziploc bag. She wanted to drive so I had to hold my beautiful grandbaby all the way to the doctors' office. Little did I know that was only the beginning of my year of hell and heartache?

The first of June 2003, my mother took ill and had to be hospitalized. She had a chronic lung disease and needed to have part of the lung removed to see if they could determine the cause of her degenerative lung disorder. I spent the entire week by her bedside tending to her every need and taking care of her. When she went home I made sure she was settled and had medical care and returned home.

The next couple of weeks were more of the same, spending night after night alone. With my husband unemployed since February I was desperate for a job. He was not looking and I could not find enough houses to clean to keep groceries on the table. The bills were piling up. We had lost our vehicle in December of 2002, the house was now in foreclosure, property taxes were past due for three years with a tax lien being processed, the telephone had been disconnected, and the lights were scheduled for disconnection.

The 26th of June I went to a nursing home to apply for a housekeeping job I was told about. The maintenance supervisor did not want to hire me as I had no work experience in commercial housekeeping, so I hit my knees crying and begging him to please give me a chance. I told him that if it did not work out he could let me go. He called me later that day to tell me he would give me a chance and to be their on the 28th. On the 27th of June 2003 we buried a friend of mine and I returned home to be left alone yet again.

At 4:30 a.m. on the 28th I awoke to get dressed and report for my first day of housekeeping. I spent all day scrubbing floors, bathrooms, and walls. I worked my tail off determined to show these people I could clean. At 2:00 p.m. I left work for home and received the surprise of my life when I arrived. There in my driveway trucks and trailers were backed up to the door and my husband met me halfway down the driveway. I jumped from the car we had just purchased for $400, and asked him what was going on when he told me he would talk to me when I calmed down. This was me calm!

I walked past our "friends" and stopped, telling them the only thing I could think of. I was mad as hell, scared, hurt, and feeling more alone than I ever had. I started screaming at them to be careful. I told them that they were messing with a child of the Most High God and He would get them back. I screamed at my husband to do whatever he thought God would let him get away with and that he could not do anything to me that God did not allow.

As I walked through the front door he called our daughter and told her to come over because I was going to need her. She called my neighbor who came in to find me going through empty rooms, listening to the echo, staring where pictures used to hang, and then curling up in the bedroom floor to try and figure out what I had done that was so bad that I deserved this. Not one sock was left behind of his or my sons.

As if my loneliness was not enough, I discovered even more. My husband had emptied my dirty clothes out of the laundry basket, into the corner of the room, so that he could take the basket. He took the food, the furniture, the money, and anything and everything else he wanted. He told me he would be back for the dining room set, the freezer and refrigerator. He did, however, leave the broken furniture for me.

My neighbor and I sat in that room looking around and both of us kept asking each other, "What is he doing?" She even asked me if he had lost his mind thinking he was allowed to take everything. I had no food, no furniture, no money to pay for gas for my broken down shell of a car he had just bought for $400, and no life. All I had left was me, an empty house, a car that overheated and was not safe to drive, and a $6 an hour job scrubbing shit off the floors and walls. I even had to quit school, one year shy of my degree, because the hours interfered with my work schedule.

The next day I got home from work to find my family at my doorstep. They worked on my car to get it running, bought me groceries, gave me gas money, and bought my work clothes. With the help of numerous friends I was able to borrow enough money to pay the $978 light bill (it had not been paid since March) and keep the lights on. I paid it back a little at a time until I got it paid off, but I have paid every penny back.

The remainder of the year was no better. My grandmother had a heart attack and eventually died in August. In September my daughter and her husband came to dinner and were involved in a wreck on the way home where she almost died. It was discovered at the hospital that she was pregnant with the second child. Her husband became even more abusive and she eventually lost that child in October. My uncle died, my son was hit by a car where he lived with his father, my cousin died, I lost my job, the attorneys were calling to notify of foreclosure on the house due to no payments received in almost a year, the county was trying to seize the property due to three years of back taxes owed, and I had a heart attack. I was not even holding on by threads any more.

Eventually, a friend of mine called me and said that her company was hiring Medical Transcriptionists to work at home for $15 an hour and she got me an interview. I tested and was hired. This was the beginning of a long uphill climb towards my getting back up on my feet.

CHAPTER 17
SURVIVING THE DESERT

For most of us we do not always understand or recognize when we have arrived in the desert. We blame our situation on our circumstances, our upbringing, or even the choices of those in our lives. I was no different. For months I blamed my husband's choices as the reason for all that was wrong in my life. If I had a bad day it was his fault, after all, if he had not left I would not be in such dire straights.

Coming to grips with my loneliness and the physical rejection of a man I had trusted and given my soul to for all of my adult life, I decided that if I isolated myself no one could get to me or hurt me again. For months I did not go anywhere, talk to anyone unless it pertained to work, and I did not care. My thoughts were that if my husband, who was supposed to love me, could reject me and leave me alone and never look back then who else would. Maybe I did not deserve love.

I would call his cell phone to speak with my son and get denied. He would tell me that my son did not want to talk to me. I contacted the school where they lived and explained to them that I was a concerned parent and wanted to stay abreast my son's academic progress. His teachers would e-mail me with progress reports and I received report cards via the mail. For his 16th birthday, I bought him a cell phone of his own so that I did not have to go through my husband to speak with him, and my son could stay in contact with his friends. I explained to him there were no strings attached. I would hope he would use it to call me occasionally but it was his choice. I called that phone every day to leave the message that I loved him and that he could never do or say anything that would change that love. I went on to remind him that he would always have a home with me if he ever decided to return and that he could call me at any time, night or day.

I absorbed myself in work. I did not eat, did not sleep, I just worked. By day I would be fine then night would come and the walls would close in. For hours I would sit in the corner behind a piece of furniture trying to hide from the darkness. For months I was lost in a world which was not good for my health. I knew that things had to change but I did not know how to change them.

I began watching every Christian channel I could find. Sermon after sermon flooded my day. Soon I began ordering every worship CD I could find and searching for Bible studies. I became so good at the music that I soon discovered that I could listen to the dictation, type the files, and listen to the music without ever missing a beat. I had gone from one extreme to the other. God was going to answer my prayers whether He wanted to or not. I was going to make Him hear me.

I sat down and typed up a list of the things satan had

stolen from me and the things God had to give me back because I believed in Him to do it. Crazy I know but at that point I was crazy. After a while of sermons and Bible studies, and trying to force God to answer my hearts desires, I started making myself go to bed at night, at least for a couple of hours. I would crawl into that bed, pull the covers back on the empty side, and say the stupidest thing; "Jesus, You say You are my Husband so let's go. If You are my True Husband then it is time to go to bed." His Word does say that He went to the Father to prepare a place for His bride. I would pull the covers back up, turn my back to the pillow and tell Him goodnight and that I loved Him. Night after night I tucked Jesus into that bed.

Day after day I prayed for the return of my husband and son. Day after day I trusted God to restore my family. I would mail cards and letters to my husband reminding him of my love and commitment to him. I would let him know that all had been forgiven and that it was not too late to come home and help me to save our family before it was too late. Then he started coming over late at night because he wanted to talk. I would ask where my son was and would be told he was asleep. I would wake the next morning to find my husband gone and would not hear from him again for days or weeks. Each time I built myself up to be strong enough to cope with each day and was completely dependent on God for my breath, my husband would show up for the night.

When I would hear from him, I would ask what was going on and he would tell me that it did not mean anything. He was sorry that he had gotten my hopes up. The last time he came to my house in the middle of the night, he was lying next to me and I asked him if this time was different, and if he ever had any intentions of coming home. He told me he did not know. I went on to explain to him that if all I was to him was a whore then for him not to forget to leave my money on the dresser when he left. To my amazement, he got up, dressed, and without saying a word proceeded to put a $20 bill on the dresser and leave. He came back a few nights later but when he crawled in my bed that night I told him that if he touched me I would kill him. I was no man's whore!

My prayers began to change at that point. Night after night, day after day, I would pray the same prayer; "God if You are as merciful as You say You are then please give me my heart back." At that point, I did not believe that my husband deserved my love or my heart and I did not want to hurt anymore at his hands. I did not want to love this man anymore. I turned all my focus on learning to love myself, on being proud of the life I had created, and on taking all the love that God had formed within me to help others. I lived to find others that I could help.

For Thanksgiving I found a church that was having a meal for those without families and I offered my services. I baked 14 turkeys and made nine pans of cornbread dressing. I served plates to as many of those families as I could and kept their glasses filled with tea. I felt alive for the first time in months. After Thanksgiving I contacted the school where my son had previously attended and asked for names from the angel tree. I was given two names and bought presents galore for the two children who needed me. I decided that if my own two children did not want to have anything to do with me I would allow God to send me new ones who would appreciate my efforts. After all, God's Word does say that He would restore all that was taken!

For Christmas my son decided to come home to stay with me for his school break. I was in heaven. I could finally see God starting to restore and answer my prayers. I was grateful for what little I was receiving and was determined to accept as little or as much as I was given. During his visit his father became angry that I had allowed our son to visit some of his friends and cut his visit short. Eventually my son would call asking if I could pick him up for the weekend and I did. Each time he would call I would drop whatever I was doing and rush to get him.

Finally payday arrived. While my son was visiting so that he could use my computer to do some research for a school project he decided to leave a note for me to read later. His dad picked him up and for hours I sat crying before deciding to get back to work. I sat down at my desk and turned on the computer monitor to find a note that read "mom I want my room painted white. I am coming home when school is out if you will let me." My heart jumped right out of my chest that day. My son had given me the most precious gift ever in those few words. Those words gave me hope and kept me going when I did not think I had the strength to get past one more second. Eventually school did let out and he did come home.

CHAPTER 18
THE GOODNESS OF GOD

After years of struggling for a marriage which was dead, and trying to glue the pieces back together of family which were about as separated as separated could be, it was time to face the reality that maybe God had not wanted this marriage to be saved. I soon began to understand that maybe God had answered my prayers and His answer was no. As this reality began to sink in as a possibility things in my life started changing.

I began noticing that I was not as sad as I had been. The tears had stopped and I became content with what God wanted. If He hated divorce and yet He was okay with my being divorced, how could that be? I found various questions rising up within me that sent me on an even deeper journey to find answers. Why would God allow divorce and why would He want me to be divorced?

For days on end I studied on this question. If He was in this, then He could give me some incite as to why He would allow it. I began changing my prayers and spending more time reading books and Bible studies about God's view on divorce. Before long I would be reading a book, listening to a sermon, or just sitting quietly and would start to hear this quiet little voice from within me telling me of the things that had been in my past.

This voice would place a feeling within me that made me feel safe and without shame. At first I thought I had completely lost my mind but soon discovered that I was the only one hearing the voice and if it made my days better then no one else had to know. As if just knowing that did not end my journey. I began researching books on how to hear God's voice and know that it is Him.

Soon I began receiving calls from friends who were having problems within their marriages and found myself giving them the information I had learned or experienced. I would ask them what they were doing to help their mates. I would tell the men to try running a hot bath and making a quiet place for their wives to rest without being disturbed. Try cooking dinner for them and putting the kids to bed. Give the wives a night off so that they could be rested, relaxed and feel appreciated.

The women were another story. I would ask them how they showed their husbands they appreciated the things he did every day to support his family. Had they tried greeting him at the door with a hug and kiss, instead of the wrongs of the day? Give him the occasional back rub and foot massage to show your appreciation. Make short calls during the day to let him know how much he was missed.

In all my prayers and efforts to save my own marriage I began to realize that all these others were now in very loving marriages and mine was still a shamble.

On one occasion I sat down and began to cry harder than ever before. I started screaming at God, through my tears, telling Him how unfair it was that I could save everyone else's marriage and He could not or would not save mine. I will never forget what that incredible voice said to me. In my devastation, I heard these words, "Was this My marriage for you or was it yours?" That was a question I had not thought of so I began praying that I would get the answer.

Days went by before I heard that voice again but when I did it was not without recourse. We often wonder why God allows things to happen. Why does He not stop them? The truth I have learned is that it is not that He does not stop them; it is more that He cannot. From the very first time that I met my husband that same voice was there within me. I can remember that feeling that I needed to play it safe and run from this situation. I chose to turn a deaf ear.

I believe that God cannot or does not prevent things in our lives because of the free choice He has given each of us. We all feel those warnings and we all feel that place from deep within us, but we choose not to listen. In most cases it is because we do not know what it is and choose to ignore that gnawing at our gut. Reality for me was that I had chosen this man as my husband, not God. That God driven gnawing at my gut, warning me not to get involved, was my spirit telling me to leave this one alone. God could not keep a marriage together which was not His choice for me.

With this new found revelation I stopped fighting my husband's divorce. It was eventually granted and I found myself divorced and more lost and full of questions. What would come of me now? Would I be the woman at the well the Bible speaks of where Jesus asked her where her husband was and she told him she did not have one. His answer back was "you're right, you have had five." How was I ever going to stand before God on judgment day and tell Him I had no husband? How would I ever explain how I had failed at the one thing that is closest to God's own heart? Where did I fit into His plan for my life now that I was a tainted woman?

One night while sleeping harder than I had in years I had the strangest dream. I was mowing my now ex mother-in-laws yard and there was a man, with a blackened out face, sitting on a tractor, mowing the far corner of the yard. My ex-husband drove up and was angry and screaming at me that some man was mowing his mom's yard. I looked behind me and noticed that this man was now standing behind me and telling my ex-husband that he would not allow him to yell at or speak to his wife that way.

In this dream I am standing between these two men and telling the faceless man that he was not my husband, while pointing at my ex and saying that he was. As soon as I had heard myself say those words I heard a very clear voice saying "woman behold thy husband" and a hand pointed to the faceless man behind me. Even in this dream, I was confused because I was not married to this man and had no clue who he was. What do You mean behold thy husband? For days I dwelled on this dream trying to figure out what it could have possibly meant.

Day in and day out I did not go anywhere out of fear of running in to this faceless man. I was finally content with being alone. Over the past three years, since my husband had left, I had had to face all my fears and demons so I was no longer afraid of the dark or sleeping alone. I was no longer afraid of not being able to support myself or to be happy without him. For the first time in my life I discovered that I loved me. I was not a bad person nor was I a perfect person, but I loved me and I loved that God had chosen me to endure the hardships because they made me a better person.

As life would have it, weeks went by and the job, which I had held for two years, took a turn for downsizing. Little by little the workload began decreasing and the paychecks became scarcer. I could no longer afford to work from the comfort and security of my home office. Then that fateful day came when I received my letter that my services would no longer be needed. I was forced to look for work elsewhere.

Determined to not go out into the world I spent weeks searching for any other jobs which would allow me to work from home. I loved my seclusion and the safety of being within my four walls but God had other plans. A friend of mine had just lost her job so we decided to find something where we could work together. We went to a workforce seminar and much to our surprise both of us were hired to help rebuild the towns which weeks earlier had been devastated by a hurricane.

During this time my ex-husband had been making it his life's mission to keep me upset. His mother was still living on my property so it gave him the eyes and ears he needed to keep watch over me and know my every move. He visited often and would spend hours doing everything he could to keep me miserable. When this job opened up it allowed for me to spend the majority of my time out of town, which I felt was God giving me the space I needed to heal the wrecked emotions of a divorce. With each trip out of town it would make my ex-husband even angrier because he did not know where I was or who I was talking to. He had lost control.

After a couple of months driving from state to state doing resets and cleanup a friend of my friend discovered that his company was hiring and we both applied and were accepted. It was jobs working within the construction field. She was hired to run a grout pump and me to be the cite secretary or so I thought. We showed up that Monday morning to report for work and discovered that the secretarial position was not yet ready so I was asked to learn the grout pump just in case they ever needed someone to fill in. Here I was a secretary by trade, small framed, weighing 99 pounds working as a construction worker! What was I doing here?

Day after day, I would go to work and spend my days crying within myself asking God did He not see me. Why had I been placed here and what was my purpose? I started asking Him to show me my purpose here so that I could move on. Almost on a daily basis I would have to remind the men that I was not there to find a man, I was there to earn my pay and support my son. I was happy being alone and was not there for their pleasure. All I wanted to do was perform my job to the best of my abilities and find the place where God could use me to better someone else's life, and then I could move on.

Soon I discovered truck drivers coming up to me for marital or girlfriend advice. Men who were going through divorces they did not want and trying to find emotional peace with their failures. Day after day at least one person would approach me and want to talk about God or healing. Eventually my friend told me that the man who had gotten us hired was going through some problems and needed someone to talk to. She continued telling me that I would be the best one to talk to him because of what I had just been through.

What could it hurt? Sure I would sit down and talk with him; after all, I was the queen of saving everyone else's life. It was my own life that I could not save. The three of us went to dinner that night. We laughed, told stories, and had a great time. The next day she told me that he did not feel comfortable talking in front of her and wanted me to go to dinner with him alone that evening. At first I said no because I did not want him to think of it as a date. After a while of thinking about it I told him that I would go to a public place with him as long as he understood that I was not looking for anyone, and that it was not a date. I was told that he was going through some things, that he needed someone to talk to, and that I would be able to help him because I had been through similar things.

We went to dinner and spent the entire night talking. It was nice because I felt so comfortable being around him and knew that I did not have to worry about advances or being attacked by him. I had learned things about him that night that my friend did not even know. Why in all the years she had been friends with him did she not know that he was an ordained pastor who left his church due to his anger with God over the loss of a child? Following the loss of his son, his wife filed for divorce. He did not feel worthy of the ministry due to his own failures.

For years he fought God at every turn and eventually turned completely away from Him. He found himself living in bars and eventually met and married a woman he knew God did not want him with. Now here he was lost in a loveless marriage and so out of God's will for his life that he was miserable. She was an unbeliever and did not want him speaking God's name much less going to church or witnessing to anyone. For years he went on this way until God began to pull him back. His wife eventually filed for divorce and he found himself alone again.

For weeks we talked and eventually he began praying again. I explained to him that if God had called him to preach and to teach that He would not allow him to stray too far. I told him to ask God in his prayers what He wanted him to do. That although God had not healed his son the way he wanted Him to, it did not mean that He did not heal him. His son had been dead for more than sixteen years and this man had never gone back to his son's graveside. I went with him to visit that graveside and to find closure.

During this time my lawnmower had broken down and the grass was about waist high. I had been trying to find someone to hire to mow the yard but no one would help me because of my ex-husband. They did not want to make him angry. I had received a letter from the county stating that if the grass was not mowed within ten days they would file charges against me for creating a hazardous environment to the community. My new male friend offered to come and help me because he owned a tractor and it would take a tractor to mow it.

Excited to have the help I agreed to let him help me. He showed up and we worked all day mowing and cleaning up. I was sitting on my ex mother-in-laws porch, watching him mow, when I was consumed by fear. I saw that tractor coming from behind her house and remembered the dream I had had months earlier about the faceless man on a tractor in that exact spot, and heard that voice saying, "woman behold thy husband". I jumped up and screamed as loud as I could, "I do not think so! I am not looking for a man and this is not happening." Could this be the man God had shown me in that dream? I do not think so!

Over the next few months we continued praying together. He regained his relationship with God and for the first time in years began hearing His voice again. We attended church services, healing seminars, and Bible studies together. We had become good friends and felt this spiritual connection that from the very first day made us feel comfortable around each other. The only thing that meant to me was that God was going to use us for the ministry and that men and women could "just be friends."

One day while he was at work he called me because he had experienced something that had him in tears. He was sitting in his crane talking with God and trying to find purpose for his life. What did God want to use him for, and how could He use him at all when he was divorced and had walked away? The Spirit of God spoke to him and told him that it was time for him to return to the ministry. God continued to tell him that He had sent him a helpmate who was not afraid to do what needed to be done. I did not want to hear this! God had not told me anything. I told him that God was first in my life. I would not be out of God's will for me again. I was not marrying anyone that God did not choose for me. I was not pastor's wife material.

Over the next year ministry opportunities arose which involved the two of us. My friend regained his relationship with God and the two of us continued to minister in the workplace and surrounding communities. Our job traveled from job site to job site so we had opportunities in a number of cities. Much to my surprise it was slowly discovered that for generations back in my family tree the men in my family were pastors. My being named Deborah was no accident and my being destined for the ministry was inevitable. I had been chosen from generations back to serve in the ministry.

Today he and I are married. Life with him is the complete opposite of my first marriage. Instead of sleepless nights waiting for my husband to return from wherever it was that he had gone, to be rejected and suffering the emotional and mental abuse he inflicted, I am now married to a man who truly adores me. He values my worth and praises me for everything. Every night he sits at my feet and gives me foot massages. I tell him that it is not necessary and he reminds me that he wants to. He says it is his way to prostate himself before God in thanks of giving him a Godly wife. He calls me throughout the day or sends messages over the phone to say that he loves me or misses me. We do not argue, instead we discuss our differences, and if it is something we just cannot agree on we pick up our Bibles and pray that God will show us the right answer. We thank God every day for the gift he has given us in each other.

CHAPTER 19
FROM VICTIM TO VICTOR

I f you have managed to get this far then I pray you are receptive to the spirit that lies within you. That place deep inside that may be telling you that you are worthy of all the plans and gifts which God has waiting for you. No matter what your present situation is God can change it and bring you into a place of strength and courage; a place of joy, peace and purpose.

Please do not misunderstand me. I do not condone divorce. I do, however, believe that if you find yourself in a troubled marriage that you do everything under God's direction to make that marriage work. Be the man or woman that God wants you to be to your mate. You were not created to go through this life alone. You were also not created to be abused or mistreated. I believe that if each of us would do our parts to be the helpmate, which we were created to be, the divorce rate would be nonexistent. We would not need family court judges.

I also believe that God's Word is True in stating that before we say "I do" we confirm that we each are believers of His Ways and we each are doing our part to live our lives to Honor Him. If we are following this guideline then we would not disrespect or abuse each other. The Bible states that we are not to be unequally yoked. That means that if you are a believer, you should only marry another believer. This does not mean that if you accept Christ as your Savior after marriage that you leave your spouse. If you are already married to an unbeliever then you are to stay with them, unless they leave. If the unbeliever leaves you are to let them go.

In my circumstances my ex-husband played the part but did not truly believe or follow God's ways. The world's ways held much more fun for the lifestyle he chose to live. Regardless, I did everything by God's rules to save that marriage but was hindered by my ex-husbands lack of belief. The Bible says that if you are married to an unbeliever, he or she is covered by your salvation, but if the unbeliever leaves then you are to let them go. Like me he had the free choice to make his own decisions. Despite 26 years of pleas, prayers, hopes and dreams, he still had the freedom to choose for himself how he chose to live his life. I was the victim of those choices.

If God could take the messed up, shell of a person that I was and make this victim the victor, then how much more could He do for you. If you find yourself living a similar life as mine, do everything in your power to lean on God for your strength. Trust Him to bring you through and guide you to that place where He wants you. If you are that one who is looking for answers and you do not know God, then make the choice today to learn who He is and what He alone can do for you. The choice is yours and no one can make it for you. You are not reading this book by accident and I believe that God has called you out, through this book, to make the choice to live the life He has chosen for you. That life filled with prosperity and blessings.

CHAPTER 20
NEW BEGINNINGS FOR A NEW LIFE

I f you are ready to make the choice to live as the victor instead of the victim then I ask that you keep reading. I will also suggest that you find someone you know who lives a Godly life and ask them to mentor you. Try to find a church to start attending and get involved with Bible study groups and church socials. But most of all you must dedicate yourself, if you are not already a believer, or rededicate yourself, if you are, and start living each day to please and serve only God.

This will not be easy at first. The last thing I wanted to do was watch "church" television channels, listen to Christian radio stations, or have someone else tell me how I was supposed to feel. How could they know how I felt they were not living my life? Wrong! Every person who is living a Godly life and serving God has had their own hell to endure. Serving God is not easy and it may even bring a multitude of resentment and resistance from your friends and family. But if you are looking for answers and have decided that this is for you, and I hope you have, then you already know that your life is a mess and you have no place else to turn. You have tried everything else and nothing is working.

It is hard to live your life as a victim. The despair and loneliness is enough to drive anyone crazy. Serving God is not easy but it does give you the assurance that you will never be alone again. Even in those times when you are tired and cannot go on, He will pick you up and carry you. You will not see Him, but in time, you will begin to feel Him when He is there and you will soon learn to recognize His sweet, sweet voice when It speaks to you. With time and consistency it will get easier and then soon you will discover that there is no other way for you.

If you are ready to take this next journey towards being a victor, I will walk you through the steps of dedication or rededication of your life to God. I will try to provide you with as many of the Bible verses and advice, which helped me to get through. I will lift you up in my prayers and ask for God's presence to surround you during your journey towards Him.

My final words to you would be this: If you can survive through the life that led you to this book, and if you are tired of being tired or overwhelmed with life; if you are thinking that this life has nothing for you here, then I want you to know that I believe in you. I know that the same strength which got you this far can see you through to your victory. You are special to me but more important you are special to God and I trust that God will lift you up and see you through your journey. You are a survivor and were chosen by God to endure your trials so that He could use you to help others become victorious.

CHAPTER 21
A, B, C'S

I f you are not already a believer then you will need to start by dedicating your life to God. It is as easy as A, B, C, but must be your starting point.

1. **A**dmit that you are a sinner. The Bible says in Romans 3:23 that we are all sinners and fall short of God's glory. We are not perfect people and God knows this. After all, He made us that way. Due to our freedom of choice, we make mistakes and do things, which are not perfect. This is where His mercy comes in. We are His children and in spite of our failures, He loves us and only wants the very best for us.

2. **B**elieve that Jesus died on the cross and shed His blood for you so that you might have eternal life with Him in heaven. John 3:16 says that God loved us so much that He gave up His son to be crucified so that our sins, past, present, and future, might be covered. All we have to do is believe that it was done for us and accept that He

loved each of us that much that He gave up His only Child's life for us.

3. **C**onfess your sins. In Romans 10:9 we learn that if we confess with our mouths that we have sinned against God, believe in the Lord Jesus, and believe in our hearts that God raised Him from the dead so that each one of us might be saved, then the slate is wiped clean. I do not know if you grasp the full concept of what that means, but to me it means that God forgets anything and everything I have ever done. This however, does not give me a free ticket to continue in that sin. If I am truly repentant of my sins against God, I will strive to remove that sin from my life. I cannot live for God and continue to live my life doing what the world does.

If this is the place where you find yourself, and you are ready to take that first step to your journey towards Christ and the eternal life He offers, then repeat this simple prayer, or say your own. If you are that one who was once living for God and found yourself in things, which separated you from His love, then you too can ask His forgiveness and all will be forgotten. It does not matter because God hears your heart not your words.

Lord Jesus, I know that I am a sinner and that I have done things, which were not pleasing to You. Thank You for Your mercy and for loving me enough to send Your Son Jesus to be tortured and crucified for me so that I can be forgiven. Thank You for raising Him from death so that I might have life eternal with You in heaven. I open my heart to You now so that You can make Your place there and lead me to the path You have prepared for me. I know that I am not perfect, and that I will make mistakes, so thank You for loving me in spite of them. Amen!

CHAPTER 22
WORDS OF ENCOURAGEMENT

- Joshua 24:15 – the world thinks that it is evil to serve the Lord. It will persecute you for your choice. Your family and friends may think you are crazy and start to pull away from you. Regardless, you must choose whom you will serve. You will either serve the world or you will serve God, but you cannot serve both.
- Psalms 31 – when you make the decision to serve the Lord, your enemies will come out of the woodwork. You may not know who they are, are even think that you have them, but troubles will come. David wrote this passage when he was going through tough times of his own. He was depressed, felt alone, and ashamed. He loved God but because of his own imperfections, and the fact that David too was not perfect he was ashamed and did not feel he was worthy of God's love. David had committed adultery, sent an innocent man to war knowing he would not survive the battle, just so he could have the man's wife who was pregnant with his

child. This is David's prayer to God to give him strength and courage when he had none. He was also asking God to keep him safe from those who came against him.

- Psalms 138:7 – another of David's passages tell us of more of David's struggles with trouble. He is asking God to revive him even in the middle of his troubles. In this passage, David is telling God that he believes that He is the sword of his protection, and that without God in his life he will not survive the attacks of those things coming against him. David is trusting God to save him from these attacks.

- Matthew 5:3-12 – the beatitudes are one of the most beautiful scriptures in the Bible. While Jesus was still alive on the earth, He was giving a sermon on the mountain and seeing the multitudes of people who had gathered to hear Him, he could not help but teach of blessings. There are blessings for the meek, those in mourning, those who are hungry, and those who are suffering persecution, and so forth. As I sit here reading them now I imagine Jesus speaking those blessings straight to me. I find so much love, and so much beauty, in so few words. He loved you and me that much.

- Matthew 11:28-30 – in this scripture Jesus talks of labor and heavy burdens. He is trying to tell us that if we would lean on Him, and let Him take the reigns, we could find that place of peaceful rest. That does not say that our trials and battles will be over; it means that we will not be alone to carry the load by ourselves.

- Matthew 17:20 – Jesus knew that we would have problems believing everything that we hear or read about Him. He knew that we would have our doubts about what He could handle or provide. Here He is asking us to have only the faith of a mustard seed. If you have never seen a mustard seed, it is a tiny little seed. Take your pen and put a dot on the page and you will have just about the size of this seed. Therefore, with that in mind you can see that He is not asking for very much here.

- Philippians 4:13 – this is one that speaks of how Jesus is your strength. If He can die and be resurrected, then how much more can He handle your problems than you will be able to handle them?
- Philippians 4:19-20 – God will supply all your needs according to His riches. We have no need to want or ask for anything because God already knows what we need. Most of the time when we ask for things, it is always selfish and for material gain. In these verses, we are to ask for those things, which will profit the Kingdom of heaven.
- II Timothy 2 – enduring hardships is the key to being successful. This passage gave me strength when I could not find any. I did not always understand what it meant or even how to follow through, but I kept crying my way through reading it.
- James 1:2-3 – counting it all joy. If you are like me, then right about now you are screaming, yeah right! How are you supposed to consider those things joy when they are ripping your world apart? The testing of your faith will produce patience if you can bear through it. You will never perfect it, but things will get easier and less stressful.
- I Peter 3:17-18 – if you read this one you may ask yourself how it can be better to suffer for doing good things, than for doing wrong ones.

I do not have all the answers, nor do I expect that I ever will. What I do know is that when I discovered who Jesus truly was, and what He had sacrificed for me, I knew that just playing with salvation was not enough. He deserved better than that from me. You may ask how I know for absolute certain that the words of the Bible are true. I can only answer that by saying that I do not know for absolute certain. I have tried it my way and it did not work. What do I have to lose if I hang on to the words in this one book believing them to be true? I may or may not have anything to gain, but if they are true, I have everything to lose.

May God be with you, and may all your years be blessed and prosperous ones.